How to Start a Cargo Van and Box Truck Business?

A Simple Guide to Setting up Your Cargo Van Business

Table of Contents

Introduction

This booklet is for you if you've been laid off, outsourced, tired of intense competition, or just require more earnings and a more promising future. This booklet is for you if you're ready to take charge and be your own boss. Want to start your own CARGO VAN business to increase your profits but don't know where to start? Want to teach you quickly and practically with an effective guide written by someone with first-hand experience?

Stop: Look no further! You just found it! Here's the pact: Most people are reluctant to initiate a trucking business because they don't know where to start: Fortunately, this book will teach you everything you need to know to get started. Of course, just getting started is only half the battle. You also need to learn how to build a successful business, and this book will help you. Imagine what it's like to start your own business and finally take control of your hours and income. Pursue the approaches summarized in this booklet, and you can do just that!

Chapter # 01

How to start a Cargo Van and Box Truck Business?

Transportation is one of the considerable lucrative enterprises in the world. Also, if you plan to start small, it's easy and doesn't require much investment. However, the industry is highly competitive due to the low barriers to entry. However, to stand your ground against the competition and succeed, you must plan and manage your business and finances effectively.

1. Choose a name for your Cargo Van and box truck business

The first step in starting a box truck business is choosing your business name. That is a very important choice because your business name is your brand and will last for the life of your own business. Ideally, you choose a meaningful and memorable name. Here are some suggestions for selecting a name for your cargo van business:

Make sure the name is available. Check the name you want against the trademark database and your state's list of registered business names to see if it's available. Correspondingly, inspect if an appropriate domain name is available. Please keep it simple. The best names are usually easy to remember, pronounce and spell. Think about marketing. Choose a name that reflects your van business's desired brand and focus.

2. Develop your Cargo Van and box truck business strategy

Developing your business plan is one of the most crucial steps in forming a box truck business. Creating a plan ensures that you fully understand your market and business strategy. The program also provides a roadmap to follow and shows funding sources if needed to raise money for your firm. Your business procedure should comprise the subsequent areas:

Executive Summary - This section should recapitulate your whole business strategy so that readers can quickly understand the key details of your van business.

Company Overview - This section introduces readers to the history of your van business and the type of van business you operate. For example, are you a food delivery business, a package delivery business, or a moving company?

Industry Analysis - Here, you will record key information about the van industry—conduct market research, and document the industry's size and trends influencing it.

Customer Analysis - In this area, you will record who your ideal or target clients are and their demographics. For example, how old are they? Where do they live? What do they think is important when purchasing the products and services you will provide?

Competitive Analysis - Here, you will record the leading direct and indirect competitors you will face and how you will build a competitive benefit.

Marketing Plan - Your marketing strategy should handle the 4Ps: product, price, promotion, and location.

Product: Identify and document the product/service you will offer

Price: Record the price of your product/service

Location: Where will your business be located, and how will this location help you increase sales?

Promotions: What promotions will you use to attract customers to your van business? For example, you may decide to use pay-per-click advertising, public relations, search engine optimization, and social media marketing.

Operational Planning - You will identify the key processes to run your day-to-day operations. You will also determine your personnel needs. Finally, in this part of your plan, you'll create a projected growth timeline showing the milestones you expect to execute over the next few years.

Management Team - This area attributes the background of your firm's administration crew.

Economic Plan - Ultimately, the financial plan replies to the following questions:

- What start-up costs will you incur?
- How will your van business make money?
- What are your projected sales and expenses over the next five years?
- Do you need to raise capital to start your business?

3. Choose a legal structure for your van company

Next, you must select a lawful structure for your van enterprise and document it and your firm name with the Secretary of State in each state you work. Here are the three most common legal structures:

1. Sole proprietorship

You can structure your company in a few different ways. The simplest is a sole proprietorship. In this option, one person owns and operates the entire company and bears all its legal obligations.

Rather than filing the firm's taxes as a business, the proprietor retains them on their personal tax return. Sole proprietorships are relatively simple, so you can easily set up and register them.

The disadvantage of a sole proprietorship is the debt. If you are a solitary proprietor, you must endure any commitment yourself. If someone or a company takes legal action against your company, defending yourself will be at your own expense.

2. Limited liability Company (LLC)

A limited liability company (LLC) suggests better lawful protection than a sole proprietorship or partnership. An LLC is usually an entity separate from the owner. If someone takes legal action against your freight LLC, the results will affect your company's assets, not yours.

Applying as an LLC requires more steps and documents depending on your state. Usually, you have to expend a cost to submit these manuscripts. While it needs more work and finances to initiate, LLCs offer better protections you may need in an accident. Freight forwarding can be dangerous so you may need more legal protection.

3. C Corporation

As with LLCs, corporations require documents that outline the roles of different people within the company. A company consists of shareholders who own the company, directors who manage the company, and officers who are responsible for day-to-day operations.

To file as a corporation, your corporation usually must file articles of association and incorporation, but the requirements vary from state to state. Different taxes apply to corporations compared to other types of corporations.

Corporations are the most complex organizations regarding legal work but offer the most protection. A company may be your best option if you have multiple owners or plan to grow substantially.

Once you register your van business, your state will send you your official Articles of Incorporation. When setting up a bank account, you will need this and other documents (see below). We recommend you consult an attorney to determine which legal structure is best for your company.

4. Secure start-up capital for your cargo van and box truck business (if needed)

When developing your van business plan, you may have already identified that you need to raise funds to start your business. If so, the main funding sources for a van business are confidential savings, family and friends, credit card financing, bank loans, crowdfunding, and donor investors. Angel investors are people who fund early-stage businesses. Angel investors typically invest in a van business that they believe has much growth potential.

5. Find a location for your business

The greatest thing you must do is find a location for your business. Here are a few things to consider when choosing a location:

- Is the area accessible for trucks?

- Is there enough space to park the truck and unload it?
- Is the area safe and secure?

Once you've narrowed down your options, it's important to visit each location and see for yourself if it meets your needs.

6. Obtain Federal and State Tax IDs

Before paying sales tax, you may need to register your business with the IRS and obtain an Employee Identification Number (EIN). The EIN is the equivalent of your business' Social Security number and is required on your state and federal tax returns. (If you're a sole proprietor having no workers, you don't require an EIN. Instead, you'll file your taxes using your Social Security number.)

EIN is also required to open a business bank account and keep your business and personal finances separate.

You may also require a state tariff ID number. You must obtain an EIN before applying for a state tax identification number. Please consult your state or business attorney as the process varies from state to state.

7. Open a business bank account

Having a bank account in the name of your trucking company is essential. The process is fairly simple and includes the subsequent steps:

- Recognize and reach the bank you desire to utilize
- Assemble and submit the mandated manuscripts (usually including your company's articles of incorporation, driver's license or passport, and proof of address)
- Fill out the bank's application form and provide all relevant information
- Meet with bankers to discuss your business needs and build relationships with them

8. Acquire a business credit card

You should fetch a business credit card for your van business to help you differentiate between personal and business expenses. You should apply for an enterprise credit card through your bank or a credit card company.

When applying for an industry credit card, you must provide information about your business. That includes your business name, business address, and the type of business you operate. You'll also need to provide information about yourself, including your name, social security number, and date of birth.

Once a business credit card is approved, you can use it to produce your business purchases. You can utilize it to make your credit record, which is important for getting a loan and a line of credit for your business.

9. Obtain required business licenses and permits

You need a license to operate a box truck business. You also need a license from the Department of Transportation to operate as a commercial carrier. Depending on the truck's use, you may also need a business registration with your local motor vehicle department.

The following are the licenses and permits required for most van businesses:

- Class A license
- City business license
- state tax license
- Commercial Driver's License (CDL)
- Federal Motor Carrier Safety Administration (FMCSA) Certificate of Insurance
- Zoning and Land Use Permits: Local government zoning laws may prohibit certain business activities in designated areas.
- Building Permit: If you plan to remodel or build a commercial space, you will need a building permit.

10. Buy commercial insurance for your van truck business

Commercial insurance policies you should consider for your box truck business comprise:

General Liability Insurance: This enfolds accidents and damages to your belongings. It also covers damage provoked by your workers or products.

Auto Insurance: If an automobile is operated in your business, this insurance will cover damage or theft of the vehicle.

Workers' Compensation Insurance: If you have workers, this approach will work with your general liability policy to protect against work-related injuries and accidents. It also includes medical expenses and lost wages.

Commercial property insurance: It covers property damage due to fire, theft, or vandalism.

Business Interruption Insurance: This will cover loss of income and expenses if your business is forced to close due to a covered event.

Professional Liability Insurance: This shields your business from proficient negligence protestations.

Find an insurance agent, notify them about your business and its requirements, and they'll recommend policies that fit those needs.

11. Buy or lease suitable equipment for your van truck business

To start a box truck business, you will need some basic equipment. You will need a truck and a container to transport your cargo. You may also want to purchase a forklift or other material handling equipment to move your products more easily.

You'll also need some office equipment to keep your business running smoothly. You will need a computer, printer and other office supplies.

12. Develop marketing materials for your van business

Marketing materials are needed to attract and retain customers for your van business. The main marketing materials you will need are as follows:

Logo: Take some span to create a pleasing and acceptable logo for your van business. The logo will be printed on corporation stationery, company cards, trade materials, and more. A suitable logo can boost customer confidence and awareness of your brand.

Website: Likewise, a professional van business website provides potential customers with information about the products and services you deliver, your organization's record, and contact details. It's important to remember that the appearance of your website affects how customers perceive you.

Social Media Accounts: Create a social media account in your company's name. Accounts on Facebook, Twitter, LinkedIn, and some other social media networks will help customers and others find and engage with your van business. Build a company website, get active on social media, and connect with shippers online and in person. Attend cargo shows, social events, and business gatherings. Nurture the relationships you build and deliver great service—two reliable ways to generate referrals and referrals.

13. Buy and set up the software needed to run a van truck business

To run a van business, you need some software programs. You will need a program to track your finances, such as QuickBooks or Excel. You will also need a truck route planner and GPS for the truck.

14. Open for business

You are now inclined to initiate your box truck business. Following the stages overhead, you should be in an excellent position to construct a thriving business. Below are solutions to frequently asked queries that may assist you further.

Chapter # 02

Classification of the legal structure of the Cargo Van and Box Truck Business:

The legal form under which you set up your business can have a significant impact on:

- The way you run the action
- Operating costs
- How are you taxed?

The business structure options available to you and when they are best for your business are critical. Owner liability and income tax are two major factors in deciding which business structure to choose. The considerable standard business formats are sole proprietorships, corporations, S corporations, and limited liability companies (LLCs). Since each business structure has different tax consequences, you must choose the best structure that best suits your business needs. Contact a business service provider, such as ATBS to discuss your needs and help you choose the best option for your business.

1. Sole proprietorship

An individual owns and operates a business entity - there is no legal distinction between an owner and a business. A sole proprietorship is a small business's most common form of legal structure.

Taxes: Sole proprietorships have pass-through taxes. Businesses themselves do not file tax returns. Instead, income (or loss) is passed through Schedule C (Form 1040) and reported on the owner's tax recovery.

Liability: The proprietor of a sole proprietorship has boundless personal liability for any penalty incurred by the business. You can mitigate this threat with insurance and sound agreements.

Forming: A sole proprietorship is the most manageable mode to do business. The expense of initiating a sole proprietorship is extremely low and requires very few formalities.

Advantages of a sole proprietorship:
- Simple and fairly inexpensive to set up.
- The proprietor has indisputable authority over the business.
- One advantage of a sole proprietorship is that, unlike other business structures, your business income is only taxed once. The employer portion of self-employment tax paid can be deducted above this line, reducing your taxable income. Fitness insurance expenditures for you, your partner, and your dependents can be subtracted from your net self-employment income as an online deduction.

Disadvantages of a sole proprietorship:
- The owner has unlimited personal exposure as the owner is responsible for all liabilities arising from the business.
- Investors generally do not invest in businesses organized as sole proprietorships.
- One disadvantage of operating as a sole proprietor is that you must calculate how much self-employment tax you owe. You pay the employee and employer portion of employment tax on self-employment income, which greatly depends on your net profit. Choosing a sole proprietorship structure means you are responsible for the company's liabilities. As a result, you put your assets at risk, and they could be seized to pay off business debts or legal claims against you.
- In addition to paying your annual self-employment tax, you expect to owe at least $1,000 in federal tax in the year after your withholding and credits are deducted. Your withholding will be less than the lesser of, and you must pay the estimated tax: 1) 90% of the tax will appear on your tax return for the current year or 2) 100% of the tax liability for the previous year. The federal government allows you to pay your

estimated tax in four equal amounts throughout the year April 15, June, September, and January.

2. General partnership

A partnership is A connection between two or more persons seeking profit in a business. Partnerships can be established less formally, but since more than one person is involved, a partnership agreement should be established. The partnership agreement sets out the terms of the partnership by formalizing rules such as profit/loss sharing, percentage ownership, dissolution clauses, and management rights.

Taxation: A partnership is a tax reporting entity, not a taxable entity. Partnerships must file an annual statement retrieval (Form 1065) with the IRS to report operating income and losses but do not pay federal income tax. Profits and losses are handed to the proprietors according to the profit-sharing percentages listed in the partnership agreement. Each partner is taxed on its allocation of profit and loss.

Liability: Owners usually have unlimited personal liability. Each partner is jointly and severally liable for partnership commitments.

Formation: Usually uncomplicated to build, but it is crucial to have a lawyer create the partnership agreement. A partnership contract specifies the terms of the association and generally covers the subsequent matters:

- Contributions
- Profit/loss distribution
- Management duties
- Bookkeeping
- Banking
- Dissolution

Advantages of a general partnership:
- Relatively easy to create and maintain.
- Profits and losses are handed to the owner's tax return.

Disadvantages of a general partnership:

- Partners are privately responsible for business deficits and penalties.
- Management and oversight issues may arise without a partnership agreement.

3. Limited Liability Company (LLC)

LLC is a mix of corporations, general partnerships, and sole proprietorships. The owners of an LLC are summoned as members. Members may comprise people, enterprises, other LLCs, and foreign commodities. Most states allow LLCs to have only one owner, known as a "single member LLC."

Taxation: For tax purposes, an LLC is considered a "pass-through entity." That means that business income is passed through the business to LLC members, who document their allocation of profits or losses on their personal revenue tax retrievals. LLC entities are only required to file an information tax return, which is similar to a general partnership. A single-member LLC can report business expenses on Schedule C, E, or F of Form 1040. LLCs with more than one partner generally file a Partnership Return 1065.

Liability: LLC members are exempt from personal liability for business debts and claims, a "limited liability." If an LLC owes money or faces a lawsuit, only the business's assets are at risk. Creditors cannot obtain LLC members' personal assets unless fraudulent or illegal acts occur. LLC members are expected to exercise caution lest they "lift the corporate veil," which would expose members to personal liability. For example, LLC owners should not use personal checking accounts for business purposes and should always use the LLC company name (and not the owner's personal name) when working with clients.

Formation: To create an LLC, you must spend an application fee ($100-$800) and have articles of association at the time of entity formation. Operating agreements are admiringly suggested but not mandated in all states. Much like a partnership agreement or articles of incorporation, an LLC operating agreement sets out business ownership and operating rules. Standard operating agreements include:

- Ownership Interests of Each Member
- Member Rights and Responsibilities
- Member Voting Rights
- Profit and Loss Allocation
- Governance Structure
- Buying and Selling Terms

Advantages of the LLC structure:
- The owner has limited liability, meaning that the entity is responsible for all liabilities the company bears. • The company's profits and losses are handed to the members and are taxed only at the individual level.
- Allows an unlimited number of members

Disadvantages of LLC structure:
- Often pays additional taxes at the state level.
- Each member's share of profits represents taxable income, even if profits are not distributed.

4. Corporations (C-Corp and S-Corp)

An enterprise is the most complicated business structure. A company is a legal entity separate from the people who own or operate the company (i.e., shareholders). A company can enter into separate contracts with shareholders, but it also has certain responsibilities, such as paying taxes. Companies are generally better suited for larger established companies with multiple employees, or other factors apply (i.e., the company sells a product or provides a service that could expose the business to a lot of responsibility). Ownership is designated by issuing shares.

The two sorts of enterprises are C-Corps and S-Corps. The primary contrast between the two kinds of corporations is the tax treatment of the two entities:

Taxation (C-Corp): The C-Corp is recognized as a separate taxable entity for federal income tax purposes, so the commodity files its own tax retrieval (Form 1120). c-corporation is subject to corporate income tax (entity tax) on corporate profits. Shareholders spend personal income tax on corporation earnings distributed to owners by the company. Therefore, C-corps are subject to "double taxation."

Taxation (S- Corp): S-Corps elect to pass on corporate income, losses, deductions, and credits to their shareholders for federal tax purposes. However, entities must report income, losses, gains, deductions, credits, etc., on the form the 1120S. Shareholders of S corporations report corporation income and losses on their tax returns, subject to federal income tax at their tax rate. Therefore, the S-corps avoids double taxation.

Liability: The company is an "immortal" legal entity, which means it does not terminate upon the death of a shareholder. Company shareholders have limited liability as they are not personally liable for the debts and obligations incurred by the company. Shareholders cannot relinquish more finances than they implanted in the company. Similar to the rules for LLCs, shareholders should be careful not to "lift the corporate veil." for business purposes, Personal checking accounts should not be used, and the company name should always be used when interacting with customers.

Formation: A corporation is the creation of a more complex entity with more legal and accounting requirements and more complex than a sole proprietorship, partnership, or LLC. One of the company's main weaknesses is the board's high level of governance and oversight. When multiple shareholders or investors are often involved, this prolongs decision-making time.

Advantages of a company:

- Company shareholders have limited liability, meaning that the entity is responsible for all liabilities the company bears.
- Generally good for investors.

Disadvantages of the company:

- The process of establishing a business is more rigorous and costly.
- Gains are subject to 'double taxation, which means that gains are taxed at the entity level and the individual status when allocated to shareholders
- High level of management and supervision by the board.

Chapter # 03

How to choose your insurance?

Commercial insurance can cover specific purpose vans, whether used to transport goods, perishables, flowers, equipment, packages, or people. Personal auto insurance is designed for owners who use the vehicle for non-commercial driving, and it's important to know that if you use your vehicle for business, any accident that occurs may not be covered by your insurance. There are multiple causes why you might require retail van insurance. Here are some scenarios where you need to carry commercial van insurance:

- You own a commercial establishment and hire drivers to deliver or transport passengers.
- You operate a service-based corporation, such as a florist, bakery, or rental equipment company, and deliver to venues such as churches and reception lobbies.
- You execute a home service company, such as paint, plumbing, electrical, or carpet cleaning, and truck the equipment to the job site.
- You are a professional courier delivering documents and packages around the city using a courier truck.
- You are a commercial truck driver, working as an employee or contractor, and you use your truck to make deliveries.
- You have a van rental.
- You have a cavalcade of trucks to fascinate passengers to and from the airport.
- You provide van service to a church or nursing facility.

Commercial van insurance ensures the driver, passengers, and items and protects the business owner. For example, you can set the liability coverage of a commercial auto policy to a higher limit than a personal auto policy.

With a higher limit, you'll be able to financially protect your business operations if a hired driver is accountable for an accident that induces physical injury or property deterioration.

Business accidents can involve employees, passengers, valuables, and hazardous materials. Your commercial van insurance must cover vehicle repair and replacement costs, lost cargo, potential medical expenditures if anyone is injured, and lawful costs if the injured party files a lawsuit.

What is cargo insurance, and what does it cover?

Whether you're transporting goods by road, air, or sea, or you're in the towing business, and you need insurance for the contingencies that cause problems for your business. Despite your efforts to pack properly, your shipment may be damaged. Your vehicle could be involved in an accident through no fault. While the vehicle may be insured, this does not guarantee that the contents or materials you ship will be covered.

So, the principles are the same whether you have a fleet of vehicles or just one truck as part of your overall business to transport items. If something bad happens, adequate insurance can keep your business as usual.

Factors Affecting Cargo Insurance:

Understanding the type of cargo and trade routes is critical to how shipping affects insurance. Consideration should also be given to how the goods are packaged and ensuring that all packages are labeled for easy identification. Remember, it's best to limit the use of brand names on packages to reduce invitations to theft.

Make sure you know the route of your shipment. Traveling - which ports are involved, what the weather is like, and if there is any political situation that could affect the condition of the cargo - are just some of the questions shippers should be asking.

Benefits of Cargo Insurance:

The main benefit of cargo insurance is that it protects the shipper's investment. For a relatively small investment, cargo insurance can give you relaxation of mind.

Another advantage of cargo insurance is the maritime principle of general average, which states that all loss or damage caused by unforeseen problems is to be apportioned by the owners of the surviving cargo on the ship. Even if the shipper's cargo is not damaged, but another cargo on the ship is damaged, the shipper is still responsible for compensating the owner of the damaged or lost other cargo.

Cargo Insurance Restrictions:

There are different insurance policies, many of which will exclude coverage differently. For example, certain types of goods are excluded from covering only certain equipment and terminals, not covering damages caused by certain events, or applying only if the service is performed in a certain way.

In addition, national and international treaty limitations and the U.S. Domestic Carmack Amendment limit most carriers' monetary liability.

Shippers need to be aware that shipping providers are protected from various liabilities and should always refer to the carrier's bill of lading, duties, or other terms and conditions for specific limitations of liability.

Types of Cargo Insurance:

International and domestic transportation can be covered by cargo insurance, which is divided into:

Overland Cargo Insurance: This insurance covers all overland transportation of trucks and other small utility vehicles. Coverage includes theft, collision damage, and other related risks.

Marine Cargo Insurance: This insurance covers shipping by sea or air. It covers damage caused by cargo handling, weather emergencies, piracy, and other related issues. Also, this insurance covers international shipping.

There are several policies covering specific types of cargo when the customer is responsible for ensuring the cargo for loss or damage for a specific period (such as a year) and coverage for all luggage.

What does a commercial van insurance policy usually include?

This type of commercial auto insurance combines general liability coverage and belongings deterioration. Here's what's generally incorporated in a commercial van insurance procedure:

Personal Injury Liability: If you, an employee, or a hired driver are found at fault in an accident, personal injury liability insurance helps pay for medical bills for anyone injured in an accident, including necessary ambulance transportation.

Medical Expenses: If you/your driver and any passengers are injured in an accident, their medical expenses are covered under this medical or personal injury protection insurance.

Property Damage: If your commercial van impairs anyone's belongings (house, fence, mailbox, bike, etc.), it will cover the expenditure of a repair or alternate up to the boundaries of your policy.

Physical Damage/Collision: This portion of the policy covers any deterioration to your vehicle during an accident. It doesn't count who is accountable for the mishap.

Motorists: If you are in an accident and the vehicle at fault is uninsured or underinsured, this coverage will help cover costs that their insurance would normally cover.

Comprehensive coverage: This part of commercial insurance is for non-accident losses. It includes damage caused by natural disasters, theft, or vandalism.

Other Business Insurance to consider:

If you use a van, van, etc. for your small business, there are some other insurance policies you may want to consider:

Short tail insurance: Protects tractors without a trailer, whether dispatched or not. That is often confused with non-truck liability insurance, which covers your vehicle when you use it for personal use.

Limited depreciation coverage: Assume your automobile is proclaimed a total loss after a mishap. In that case, limited depreciation insurance can help bridge the gap between the fair market value the insurance might pay and what you owe on the vehicle or the cost of replacing it.

Mechanical breakdown insurance: Coverage is provided to assist in managing out-of-pocket costs as repairs occur.

Motor Truck Cargo Insurance: Shipping or merchandise and cargo liability insurance are provided. Among the types of commercial truck insurance, motor truck cargo insurance is an excellent option for rental truck drivers. This option can include damage due to fire, collision, or impact. Sometimes this also includes coverage to cover debris removal costs and freight to prevent further loss of damaged goods, legal defense, and customer losses.

Car carrier insurance: Protect your trucking business when you use a permanently leased independent contractor.

General liability insurance for cars and trucks: Insurance for car carriers or rental truck drivers. Covers bodily injury, bodily injury, property damage liability, advertising damage liability, medical bills, product and completed operations, and rental property damage insurance for seven days or less. The types of commercial truck coverage for motor truck general liability coverage vary by plan and provider.

Non-Cargo Liability Insurance: Covers the use of the truck for non-commercial purposes when the truck is used on a rest day.

On-hook coverage: Covers repair or replacement if the vehicle is damaged by a collision, fire, theft, explosion, or vandalism while being towed or hauled.

Optional downtime override: Coverage that goes into effect when your commercial truck is down.

Passenger accident insurance: Covers the driver in the event of an accident while an uninsured passenger is in the vehicle.

Physical damage range: Provides coverage to protect your commercial vehicle in the event of physical damage, including collisions, composites, fires, theft, and more.

Supplementary towing and cleanup: Provide additional coverage for towing operations and cleaning up contaminants and other debris.

Trailer swap agreement insurance: Provides damage insurance for non-owned trailers when they are physically damaged.

Brad and Holly of Commercial and Farmers Insurance Services understand that with so many types of commercial truck insurance to choose from, it can be overwhelming to understand what your specific situation requires. We can assist you in making an adequate selection.

If you're an owner-operator on a permanent lease to a motor carrier, you may want to consider several types of commercial truck insurance. Your specific insurance needs may depend on your lease agreement with the car carrier. Auto carriers usually offer primary liability coverage and sometimes further coverage, but you can often find better additional coverage when you're in the market with an independent insurance agent. Many types of commercial truck insurance can provide additional coverage that your primary liability insurance cannot.

What will be the cost of Insurance?

Each state has distinct prerequisites for the lowest coverage directed for commercial auto insurance. Costs also depend on your business location, driving history, claims history and vehicle miles traveled yearly. Of course, the coverage and limitations you choose for each section are also considered.

It also depends on whether you choose the " Single Claim Limit " policy or the " Split Claim Policy. " The single claim limit is the maximum payout per incident (i.e., $100,000 in bodily injury/damages). Split claims policies typically set three different dollar limits for each category: per person, total personal injury, and total property damage. For example, $35,000 per person, $70,000 in total personal injury, and $75,000 in total property damage.

How to save money on Cargo Van Insurance?

There are several ways your business can save on commercial van insurance, including:

- Need safety training for your driver
- Bundle policy with the same provider
- Hire a driver with a traffic violation/accident record

What do I need to get a commercial van insurance quote?

- To obtain an accurate commercial van quote from one of our qualified dealers: the following information is generally required:
- Contact information
- Social Security number
- Financial responsibility
- Named insured
- Vehicle year, make, and model VIN
- Diver/offending driver
- Business type
- Type of Insurance Required

Please note that your information is confidential. A Social Security number is required to verify driving and credit history and that all reported information is correct.

How to get cargo insurance?

Some carriers, brokers, and freight forwarders offer cargo insurance. Freight forwarder Alba Wheels Up is uniquely positioned to use its industry experience and purchasing volume to provide comprehensive cargo insurance at economical rates rather than high premiums, including:

Comprehensive Liability Insurance

That covers the cost of imported goods, including total duties, terminal charges, and loss of income allowances.

Door-to-Door Insurance Choices

Alba Wheels Up will file assertions and comprise statements that automatically provide visibility and details, so shippers continuously comprehend when and what to predict.

Conclusion:

Increased risk of cargo being delayed, damaged, lost, or stolen. Shippers can mitigate these risks by purchasing the right cargo insurance. While not necessarily required, cargo insurance can give you peace of mind and protect your shipper's investment. However, the benefits come with limitations, and shippers must be aware of these drawbacks.

Freight forwarder collaborations such as Alba Wheels Up will ease any uncertainty and resolve any unknowns that shippers may have. Alba Wheels Up's industry experience and purchasing volume allow this freight forwarder to provide cargo insurance explanations to satisfy the requirements of its customers.

Chapter # 04:

Where can I find the load for the Cargo Van and Box truck Business?

As a van owner, there are plenty of opportunities to put your vehicle to work and earn some hard-earned money. Where do you start?

Finding a van, straight truck, or pickup load can be demanding and time-consuming, but it doesn't have to be. Once your business is ready, you only need one thing: customers. Fortunately, connecting with shippers and brokers has never been easier.

Start with Loading Board, an online marketplace for freight and carriers. Examples include Landstar (free, premium services available for a fee) and DAT (subscription based). These load boards allow you to filter jobs by type, so you can easily find box truck jobs. Amazon Relay is a load board designed for FBA and can provide truckers with plenty of opportunities.

Another option is to use the in-stock shipping feature on an Electronic Recording Device (ELD). These ELDs are digital systems that ensure compliance with the FMCSA's hours of service rules, which govern working and rest periods for truck drivers. Many truck drivers do not need to use an ELD; service hours regulations include exceptions for short local drives. But many ELD providers offer additional freight services. The system knows your truck's location and can match you with jobs on the spot. Services like this turn the carrier into something like an Uber driver. Just open the app and start hauling.

Whether you're a truck driver or an owner-operator running a trucking business, finding loads for extra work can be daunting.

Many van owners rely on traditional loading boards to find work. Unfortunately, these boards are filled with competing drivers who compete with each other for the best jobs. Some load boards also contain limited information and fraudulent activity that undermines their trustworthiness.

Let Go Share locate loads for you! Go Share eradicates the aggravation of utilizing standard load boards with its proprietary technology. Go Share automatically lists available loads near you by connecting individuals and businesses with local pickup, van, and van owners.

Through Go Share 's numerous partnerships with local businesses and retailers, demand for the Cargo Sprinter van is always there. Some businesses may need assistance with middle-mile and last-mile deliveries to support their operations. Alternatively, some may seek help with moving and furniture delivery. Go Share matches you with these projects in real-time, and you can choose to accept projects that interest you.

The Go Share app makes it easy to keep up to date with new loads. Whenever a recent task is initiated, a stimulant message is transmitted to all regional drivers. Avoid dealing with drivers who haggle or cripple you. The first person to take the load fetches it. Projects can plan in advance, but many are time-sensitive hot appointments and same-day delivery tasks that perfectly match your schedule.

How does the owner-operator find the load?

One of the industry's most important skills is learning to find loads, especially for self-employed or small fleets. That can be a time-consuming job. But mastering this skill can be very rewarding with the right methods and tools. Here are some tips for finding the right load for owner-operators.

1. Find a freight forwarder

Freight brokers are one of the typical modes of connecting truck drivers with shippers. They can rescue owner-operators with a lot of struggles as they do most of the work matching the driver's load.

Of course, their services are usually charged, so owner-operators must be aware of any extra charges. Additionally, as brokers often negotiate rates with shippers, shipowner-operators need to take the time to assess in advance whether loading is profitable or not.

2. Negotiate the contract directly with the shipper

Signing an agreement directly with the shipper can be a good way to get the goods. That will most likely require some cold calls.

In other words, you need to contact the shipper, introduce yourself, and find out if a private contract is possible. Calls take time. Don't be surprised if most of the people you talk to reject you. This is normal for any type of cold call. However, suppose you do your homework and find local shippers who may be in the market for a dedicated driver. In that case, you are more likely to explain owner-operator load factors and create a steady stream of business.

One caveat, though. Shippers will act in their best interests, just like any business. They may sign up with more drivers than they need, so they never have a load without drivers. You may require diversifying your business across numerous shippers to guarantee business steadiness.

3. Become a government contractor

Local, state, and federal administrations all have their own transportation needs. An owner-operator can find loads by choosing to become a government contractor.

Unlike other types of loads, you must first be registered as a government contractor to be able to transport their loads. On the other hand, you can work with another company that already has a government contract. If you are interested in fulfilling a government freight contract, contact your state or municipality for more details.

4. Use Truck Loading Plates

That is presumably the most manageable and efficient mode for truck drivers to find loads.

Truck loading boards show you exactly what needs to be transported, its location, destination, weight, and other job-specific details.

Owner-operators can quickly decide, provide the shipper with rates and other details, and hit the road.

Benefits of Truck Loading Boards:
The trucking industry has always relied on truck loading boards. Initially, truck loading plates can be found at truck stops. In recent years, loading truck boards have been digitized and available on your computer or mobile phone.

- The major benefits for owner-operators, carriers, and fleet managers using advanced electronic truck loading boards:
- Truck loading plates can speed up finding loads for owner operators and fleet managers.
- In many cases, they can help the new owner-operator do business faster. They find truck loads that match their location and equipment.
- Load boards open up prospects in areas of the country where loads may not have previously been found.
- Loading boards can reduce empty loads by allowing owner-operators to book their next load in their current destination area.
- Some load boards allow owner-operators to negotiate prices.
- The load board provides the driver with flexibility in driving and work schedules.

Chapter # 05

What is the best Cargo Van/ Box Trucks?

Some reasons why you need to choose a cargo van for your business:

Save fuel!

When choosing a van, you must choose a very fuel-efficient one that will not only aid the environment but you'll also acquire adequate mileage for less money. In a competitive environment, many van manufacturers take fuel efficiency very seriously, with some vans boasting a range of 22 miles per gallon. Most vans available today are more efficient, and many of them rival large sedans.

Reliability!

With so many well-known brands to choose from, you always know that when choosing a van, you'll get a state-of-the-art van that meets all the criteria. This van can outlast most other vans if you keep up with repair services.

Brand!

You can easily have the right mobile billboard for your enterprise! Select a straightforward design, but make certain the logo is easy to see. Instead of spending a fortune to advertise outside, like on a billboard in a busy area, you're showing your company to everyone passing by every time you're on the road. So, hold the message brief and charming, so it's easy to remember while others drive!

Custom made!

Both interior and exterior can be customized. You can transform the van to be comfortable and practical as needed.

Space!

Full-size vans are spacious, averaging 120-200 cubic feet of space. That makes filling the van with more supplies easy so you can be prepared for any situation.

Comfortable!

Most commercial vehicles are uncomfortable, but full-size vans have the comfort of an SUV or minivan. And also has storage and transport potential for commercial vehicles.

Now that you have several factors to consider when choosing a van, we need to discuss which ones should make the top 8. We have considered everything and considered the most important thing - your advice. The vans detailed downward are the ones most repeatedly suggested by HVAC business owners, but their advice definitely applies to contractors from all walks of life.

Which businesses typically use vans? Florists, musicians, plumbing and HVAC professionals, caterers, painters, puppy daycare or grooming professionals, and more. If you're considering pursuing these career options, be sure to expect the added cost.

Before buying your next van, ensure you buy a quality vehicle that meets your trade needs. Here's a rundown of ten van models you might consider and what actual business owners say about them:

Ford Transit Connect van:

The Ford Transit Connect Van is a universal commercial automobile for different small businesses. Its ample cargo area can be configured for myriad jobs, from catering to electrical repairs. The Transit Connects smooth conveyance and exceptional fuel thrift make every day driving a breeze, along with user-friendly infotainment and safety features. It also makes good business sense, is inexpensive, and Ford has a great reputation for repairs. The Ford Transit Connect Van automobile has 2-seats with two trim levels. The most popular model is the XL with symmetrical rear doors LWB, which starts at $31,760 with the 2.0-liter I4 engine and front-wheel drive. This Transit Connect Van is expected to deliver 24 MPG in the city and 27 MPG on the highway.

Advantage
- The large cargo area in a small frame

- Standard driver assistance technology
- Easy to drive every day
- Excellent fuel consumption

Shortcoming
- Some vans can carry more cargo
- Basic trim lacks some amenities

Ram Prom aster City Van:

Ram Prom aster City Cargo Van automobile has two seats available in 1 trim level. The most popular model is the Tradesman, which starts at $32,270 with the 2.4-liter I4 engine and front-wheel drive. This Prom aster City Cargo Van is expected to deliver 21 MPG in the city and 28 MPG on the highway.

Mercedes-Benz Metris van:

The Mercedes-Benz Metris Cargo Van automobile has 2-seats available in 1 trim level. The most popular variant is the 126-inch wheelbase with a standard roof, which starts at $36,195 and comes with a 2.0-liter I4 turbo and rear-wheel drive. This Metris van is expected to deliver 19 MPG in the city and 23 MPG on the highway.

Ford Transit van:

Balancing cost, comfort, and performance, the Ford Transit Cargo Van offers buyers and businesses an affordable blank canvas. It has expansive cargo space, high towing and towing limits, powerful V6 power, and optional all-wheel drive. A van price starting at $40,000 should have additional standard characteristics, but Transit's solid list of driver-assistance and safety tech is a solid bet. The Ford Transit Cargo Van motorcar has 2-seat in 3 trim levels. The most popular model is the T-250 130" mid-roof 9070 GVWR RWD, which starts at $43,440 with a 3.5-liter V6 and rear-wheel drive.

Advantage
- Great towing and towing capacity
- The quiet and comfortable interior is a notch above expectations from a work car

- Spacious cargo space

Shortcoming
- The shortlist of standard features makes the base model a bit pricey
- Some competitors offer more options for specific businesses and applications

Mercedes-Benz Sprinter van:

The Mercedes-Benz Sprinter Van is a 2-seater vehicle available in 5 trim levels. The most popular model is the 2500 Standard Roof 144" V6 4WD, which starts at $55,115 with the Diesel 3.0L V6 Turbo engine and four-wheel drive.

Ram Prom aster van:

With its reasonable price and great features, the Ram Prom aster van makes a lot of sense as a work vehicle, a compact motorhome, or something in between. Most of its more promising characteristics are optional, which counts to the expense, but as a ground platform, it's a deal. The Ram Prom aster Cargo Van automobile has 2-seat available in 3 trim levels. The most popular model is the 2500 High Roof 159", which starts at $46,045 with a 3.6-liter V6 and front-wheel drive

Advantage
- Smooth V6 engine and nine-speed transmission
- Impressive towing and towing capacity
- Unlimited, customizable interior and cargo areas

Shortcoming
- Many standard driver security assets are optional, not standard
- Lack of optional all-wheel drive

Chevrolet Express Van:

A 1990s-time capsule, the Chevrolet Express is a full-size van that has been on the market for 27 consecutive years. It didn't change much back then, and business owners loved it. The Express is as tough as they are, with a durable powertrain that's easy to handle and a

10,000-pound towing capacity. Behind the driver and passenger seats is a massive cargo room with up to 284 cubic feet of space. Most rival vans are more modern and tech-focused, but Chevrolet's cargo truck is everything you need without the frills. The Chevrolet Express Cargo Van automobile has 2-seat available in 1 trim level. The most popular model is the 2500 SWB, which starts at $34,695 with the 4.3L V6 and rear-wheel drive.

Advantage
Sturdy frame. User-friendly controls. Configurable cargo area. Excellent towing capacity.

Shortcoming
Gas engines have the poor fuel economy. Cumbersome handling. Ancient technology. All-wheel drive is not available.

GMC Savana Vans:

The GMC Savana Cargo Van automobile has 2-seat Available in 1 trim level. The most popular model is the 3500 SWB, which starts at $37,795 with a 4.3L V6 and rear-wheel drive.

Chapter # 06

Will you Need MC and DOT for your Cargo Van/box truck business?

What is a dot number?

A DOT number is like your trucking company's driver's license. You can obtain a DOT number to verify with FMCSA that your company is operating as a trucking company.

DOT numbers are often used to verify that you are using the vehicle commercially, whether you are hauling your own product or moving equipment with a qualified commercial motor vehicle.

What is an MC number?

The MC number is also known as the operating authority or shipping authority. Operational authority is most often required when you plan to trade interstate (shipping goods across multiple states) or hazardous transport materials.

MC numbers are additionally costly than DOT numbers and demand a $300 fee as specified by the FMCSA.

Do box trucks require authorization?

Yes, vans require operational authorization from the Federal Motor Carrier Safety Administration (FMCSA) to cross borders or carry cargo for delivery.

Authority to operate is a mandatory requirement for any vehicle over 10,000 GVW that will or is expected to cross state lines. To do this, you need an official license from USDOT.

Your box truck business needs MC and DOT numbers. Many people don't know why having DOT and MC numbers is important. DOT stands for Department of Transportation. A DOT number is a federal registration number that identifies your business, just like your state-registered business name, with a SIC code (Standard Industry Code) and a federal tax identification number (EIN).

A DOT number does not replace your business or physical DOT address. A DOT Number is like Google My Business (GMB) that identifies your business to Google, and a DOT number guarantees that your enterprise is documented with the federal administration.

MC stands for Motor Carrier, which represents Commercial Vehicle Operator; this comprises any kind of vehicle employed for commercial objectives by a person who uses the vehicle to transport property or passengers for payment. In this matter, DOT and MC are identical.

DOT numbers and MC numbers are the identification numbers you need to run your company.

You can't request DOT and MC numbers earlier when starting a trucking company because DOT requires your actual physical address from your state DOT.

DOT requires that you have a physical DOT address before any DOT numbers are issued to you. So, if your firm is labeled new and you're unsure where to acquire your DOT number, obtain a PO Box or private mailbox with an address to give to the DOT agency number when applying for DOT.

How to Get a Trucking Authority?

Applying for a shipping authorization allows your company to obtain a license from the U.S. government to collect shipping charges as an independent company. You will obtain your authorization from FMCSA in the form of an MC number. Please follow this shipping authority checklist to ensure the registration process is as smooth as possible.

- Register your shipping company
- Get an EIN
- Get your USDOT number

- Apply for your MC number
- Submit BOC-3 and get an insurance policy
- Pay your HVUT
- Set up your International Registration Program (IRP) and get your assigned license plate
- Build an International Fuel Tax Agreement (IFTA) account
- Complete the Unified Operator Registration (UCR)
- Join a drug and alcohol complex

Chapter # 07

How to select a suitable freight factoring company?

It is noteworthy to select a factoring corporation that specializes in the freight industry, showing that the company constantly strives to keep the technology updated to help its customers.

With so many factoring companies providing financial services to trucking companies, it makes it more difficult to determine which attributes you should consider when choosing a factoring company for your trucking business.

Choose an experienced freight factoring company that understands your company. capital has been in business for around 25 years, delivering low-cost financing solutions to the transportation industry to improve cash flow. Our cost-effective factoring services are easy to use, understand and manage.

A dedicated account manager ensures you receive exceptional customer service. You'll get trusted advice from industry-experienced staff to help you make credit decisions, expedite financing and answer all your questions. Our professional truck factoring services include fuel discounts, access to an exclusive network of brokers, and free credit search tools to reduce risk and maximize your bottom line.

Why should your Box Truck business use freight factoring?

Factoring is an invoice sold to a third party (factor or factoring company) at a small discount in exchange for instant money. This economic transaction eliminates the need to wait more than 30, 60, or 90 days for your customers to pay and unlock the money you've already earned. You can instantly put the funds to pay your bills and keep your truck moving.

Factoring invoices is a common business practice in many industries because of the many economic benefits it can bring. Freight factoring is a special form of factoring designed for the transportation enterprise. It is regarded as a mainstream economic opportunity for trucking corporations to accelerate cash flow and benefit from additional cost-saving services.

How can factoring help freight companies?

Most corporations fail because of a deficiency of working capital or cash flow issues. While it's true that considering an invoice will cost you a percentage, it's usually worth the cost. The time you spend preparing bills, collecting invoice payments, and managing paperwork can be focused on moving more loads and making more money.

The time saved by having someone else track down your invoices and the paperwork that goes with them is invaluable. The more you grow, the more billable work you have. The ability to outsource it to others keeps your cash flow healthy.

The Benefits of Invoice Factoring for the Freight Industry

In addition to providing quick cash, factoring companies are credit analysis and invoice collection experts. When you work with a reputable freight factoring company, you can focus on growing your business, and the factoring company can improve your collections and reduce your credit threat. Freight factoring corporations suggest online techniques that permit you to submit invoices, follow customer charges in real-time, and confirm customer credit statements. Fuel discount programs can protect expenditures. No issue how large or small your freight corporation is, invoice factoring can contribute to your success in many ways.

Get paid faster: The factoring process allows you to get cash quickly. Freight factoring allows you to cover short-term operating costs without waiting or worrying about collections.

Overcoming Credit Challenges: When evaluating invoices, factoring companies will focus on the creditworthiness of the broker or shipper, not your credit rating. So, if your shipping business records any credit flaws, you can still get cash quickly.

Pay directly to the gas card: The best factoring companies will pay the invoice directly to the gas card and offer discounts to those in the trucking industry.

How to choose the best factoring company?

With too many factoring enterprises out there, choosing can be a challenge. When it comes to finding a funding partner for your business, finding the right one is very important. Factoring services can be an easy and convenient way to get working capital, but only if you choose a truck factoring company that works well with your organization and customers. Use the following checklist to assist you in choosing the best factoring company for your trucking business:

Integrity:

- Do freight factoring companies offer fully transparent online accounting and regular reporting?
- Are factoring rates easy to understand and easy to calculate?
- Do factoring services come with hidden fees or surprises?
- Are there any potential delays in the fundraising procedure?

Reputation
- Review the factoring corporation's website for examinations, testimonials, or case studies.
- Ask the factoring company for reference materials. Talk to their existing customers (your truck driver peers) and ask about their satisfaction.

Excellent consumer service
- Is their customer support service quick and worthwhile?

- Does factoring include dedicated account managers working directly with clients and simplifying service?
- Does the factoring company intercommunicate with you and your customers courteously and professionally?

Experience
- How long has the insurance firm been in the trade?
- Do factoring companies really understand freight. Not just from a lender's perspective but from actual, hands-on experience?
- How soon can I receive payment after submitting an invoice? Answers should be within 24 hours.
- Which invoices can I consider, and which ones are ineligible? This may depend on your customers and their credit scores, so have a checklist ready.
- Can I consider some invoices and not others? Usually, you can, but make sure. Some companies require you to consider every invoice.
- How much can I borrow at any time?
- What is your factoring fee? Preferably a flat fee. Good factoring companies often offer discounts or low rates if you consider more invoices.
- Are there other fees I should be aware of? (Remittance, Mortgage, etc.) Before signing any agreement, make sure you are aware of these fees and that they fit within your budget.
- Is there a long-term contract? If so, how long does it endure, and what are the terms? Is there a termination fee?
- What occurs if the customer does not deliver the invoice within a reasonable time? What is the time frame for the customer to pay the invoice? Do you charge an "adjustment fee" if a customer takes longer to pay?
- Do you need a reserve account?
- Is there a factoring fee for the transaction, such as sending money to my account? Is there a minimum quantity fee?

- Do you offer recourse or non-recourse financing? Recourse loans offer lower fees, but you'll have to refund the payment if the customer doesn't pay. For non-recourse loans, if the customer does not pay, the factoring company will take all risks and will charge a higher shipping factoring fee.
- How long have you been in business? Do you have experience working with a trucking company of my size?